WHO? WHAT? WHY?

WHAT IS
BREXIT?

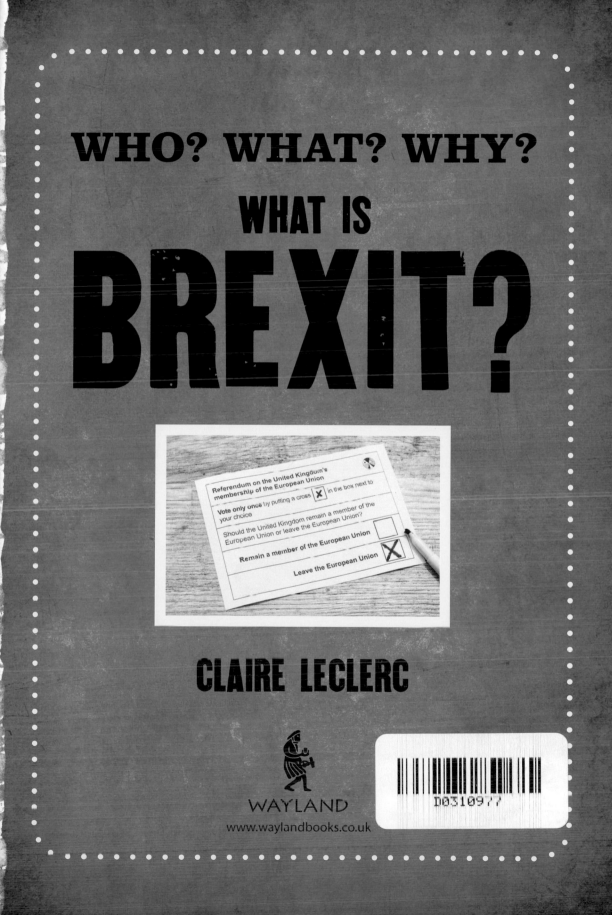

Referendum on the United Kingdom's
membership of the European Union

Vote only once by putting a cross ☒ in the box next to
your choice

Should the United Kingdom remain a member of the
European Union or leave the European Union?

Remain a member of the European Union ☐

Leave the European Union ☒

CLAIRE LECLERC

WAYLAND
www.waylandbooks.co.uk

First published in Great Britain in 2017 by Wayland

ISBN 978 1 5263 0670 8
10 9 8 7 6 5 4 3 2 1

Wayland
An imprint of
Hachette Children's Group
Part of Hodder & Stoughton
Carmelite House
50 Victoria Embankment
London EC4Y 0DZ

An Hachette UK Company
www.hachette.co.uk
www. hachettechildrens.co.uk

A catalogue for this title is available from the British Library.

Printed in China.

MIX
Paper from
responsible sources
FSC
www.fsc.org FSC® C104740

Produced for Wayland
by White-Thomson Publishing Ltd
www.wtpub.co.uk
Editor: Rachel Cooke
Designer: Dan Prescott, Couper Street Type Co.

Picture acknowledgements:
Alamy Stock Photo: AF archive 6, Trinity Mirror/Mirrorpix 9, Martyn Evans 26, Zoonar
GmbH 41; Creative Commons: 7, 29; Getty Images: Jasper Juinen/Bloomberg 10, Matt
Cardy 14, Luke MacGregor/Bloomberg 17, Jeff Spicer 25, BuzzFeed News/Facebook 27
(bottom), Dan Kitwood 32, Geoff Caddick/Stringer 33, Pablo Blazquez Dominguez 35,
Luke MacGregor/Bloomberg 38, Jack Taylor 42; iStock: narvikk 3, Clubfoto title page
and 4, whitemay 40; Shutterstock: JJFarq 5, Irina Borsuchenko 8, Pyty 11 (both), Ivonne
Wierink 12, Rotislav Kral 13, Tim M 15, Marina Pleshkun 16, Maks Narodenko 18, Kostas
Koutsaftikis 19, David Muscroft 20 (centre), Stuart Boulton 20 (bottom), MediaPictures.
pl 21 (top), JmitchellPhotog 21 (centre top), Ms Jane Campbell 21 (centre bottom), Drop
of Light 21 (bottom), John Gomez 22, Lenscap Photography 23, lazyllama 24, Lenscap
Photography 27 (top and centre), 1000 Words 28, Edward Crawford 30, Complexli 31,
Nick Beer 32 (both), Koca Vehbi 36, Ms Jane Campbell 37, R.Nagy 39, 1000 Words 43,
melis cover and 47.
All backgrounds and design elements: Shutterstock

CONTENTS

WHY DO WE TALK ABOUT BREXIT?

On 23 June 2016, Britain voted in a referendum for Brexit. 'Brexit' is short for 'British Exit' – Britain leaving the European Union, or EU. Over the next few years, this decision will make a difference to the lives of everyone living in Britain.

A DECISIVE VOTE

The Brexit referendum took place 43 years after Britain joined the EU. During that time, the EU has gradually come to have more and more of an impact on every aspect of life: from the food we eat to how we work, from where we can live to how we can travel. Nearly everything we buy is affected by rules made by the EU.

DIVIDED BRITAIN

The arguments about whether or not to stay in the EU were very heated. Feelings were running particularly high because the decision was taken by a national referendum – for only the third time in British history. Laws are usually made in Parliament by elected representatives (MPs); in a referendum, the decision is taken directly by individual voters. Many people celebrated the result, but others were left upset and fearful about the future.

A voting paper from the Brexit referendum: the question was simple – Remain in the EU or Leave? 33 million people took part.

Referendum on the United Kingdom's membership of the European Union

Vote only once by putting a cross [X] in the box next to your choice

Should the United Kingdom remain a member of the European Union or leave the European Union?

Remain a member of the European Union [ ]

Leave the European Union [X]

TAKING A RISK

Over the next two years, Britain and the EU will have to agree on a new relationship. We don't know yet whether that will be a close relationship (a 'Soft Brexit'), or whether Britain and the EU will fail to fail to reach an agreement – a so-called 'Hard Brexit'. If they don't make a deal, it could be expensive and difficult for all the EU countries, but especially for Britain. Europeans living in Britain and British people living abroad will be particularly affected. But prices, jobs, taxes, travelling abroad and healthcare may change for everyone.

SEEING BOTH SIDES

It is sometimes difficult to know who to believe about Brexit: either those who are sure it will be a good thing for Britain, or those who think it will lead to disaster. Or maybe it will be something in between? This book tries to give all sides of the story and gives the opinions of those in favour of Brexit as well as those against.

A NEW WORD

Brexit is actually a very new word, first used in 2012. It was adapted from 'Grexit' or 'Greek exit' from the EU (which was discussed but never happened). By 2016, 'Brexit' had been chosen as Word of the Year!

Has Brexit cut Britain off from the rest of Europe? Or will there still be strong connections in the future?

WHY DID BRITAIN GET INTO EUROPE?

In 1945, at the end of the Second World War, Europe lay in ruins with 40 million of its people dead. The continent was occupied by American and Russian soldiers and faced an uncertain future.

A NEW EUROPE

Even in this chaos, a small group of visionaries were already working on ways to prevent Europe ever going to war again. Amongst them was the new Italian Prime Minister, Alcide De Gasperi, the French Foreign Minister, Robert Schuman, and Konrad Adenauer, once imprisoned by Hitler but now the leader of the newly formed West Germany. At the end of the war, Germany had split in two: East and West Germany. East Germany was firmly under the control of Communist Russia but democratic West Germany was keen to build bridges with its European neighbours.

CHURCHILL'S VISION

It was, however, the great British war leader Winston Churchill who best expressed the new idea of Europeans working together to prevent future wars. As early as 1946, he called for a 'United States of Europe' although Churchill didn't think Britain needed to be part of this union because it still had its empire and strong links with the USA. Despite Britain's stance, Churchill is viewed alongside the likes of De Gasperi, Schuman and Adenauer, as one of the 'founding fathers of the European Union'.

MAY 1946

Winston Churchill and Robert Schuman. European politicians welcomed Churchill's advice after the war.

CHANGING VIEWS

When six countries, including France, Italy and Germany, set up the European Coal and Steel Community (1951) and then the European Economic Community (or the EEC, 1957), Britain stood aside. But at the start of the 1960s, the world was looking very different. Britain was losing its empire as countries gained their independence. It was obvious that other European countries were rebuilding their economies more quickly than Britain. In 1961, the Conservative government decided to apply to join the 'Common Market' as the EEC had become known.

The map shows the founding states of the EEC (European Economic Community).

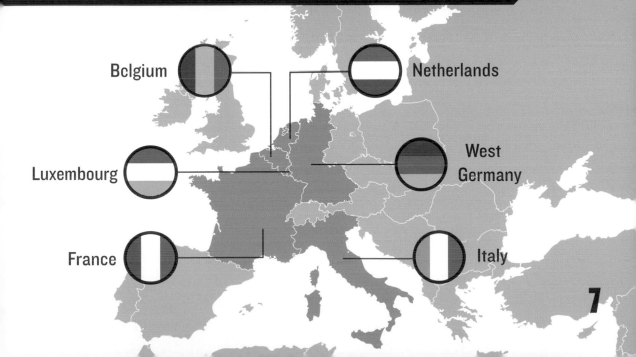

Belgium

Netherlands

Luxembourg

West Germany

France

Italy

DE GAULLE SAYS 'NON'

The French President, Charles de Gaulle, was suspicious of Britain's application. He felt that Britain would not fit into the EEC and would try to change the way it worked. He believed that the Americans wanted to control Europe via their British allies. In 1963, he rejected the British move to join.

Britain's Labour government tried to join again in 1967. Again de Gaulle said 'Non!'

ACCESS TO THE COMMON MARKET

By 1970, the UK's need for easier access for British goods to the markets of the six fast-growing countries in the Common Market was urgent. After several economic crises, the sense that Britain was slipping behind was growing.

Changes of leadership helped Britain this time. De Gaulle stood down as French President in 1969. And Edward ('Ted') Heath won the 1970 election for the Conservatives in Britain. By 1972, Heath had made a deal for Britain to enter the Common Market and the country officially joined the EEC on 1 January 1973.

↑ A statue of Charles de Gaulle, Second World War resistance leader and later French President. He twice stopped Britain from joining the EEC in the 1960s.

WILSON GOES FOR A VOTE

Not everyone was happy with Heath's deal. In particular, the Labour Party was bitterly divided: for example, many felt membership of the EEC would put up food prices. To keep the peace within his party, Labour leader Harold Wilson promised to renegotiate the terms of Britain's entry and then put membership of the EEC to a referendum.

BRITAIN VOTES 'YES'

Wilson won the 1974 General Election and carried out his promise: the vote was held on 5 June 1975.

The campaign for the 1975 referendum was one-sided and very different from the 'Brexit' referendum 41 years later. The 'Yes' side had much more money to spend on persuading voters, the support of nearly all the newspapers and the backing of business. The general feeling was that Britain was in decline and had become 'the sick man of Europe'. The EEC offered a way out – some people even talked about a 'lifeboat'. The 'Yes' side won the referendum easily and Britain stayed in Europe.

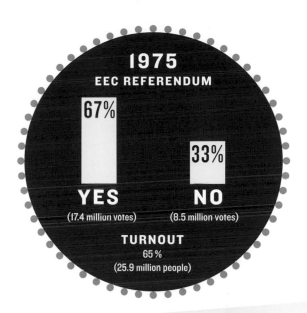

1975
EEC REFERENDUM

67%
YES
(17.4 million votes)

33%
NO
(8.5 million votes)

TURNOUT
65%
(25.9 million people)

Former British Prime Minister Edward Heath goes to vote in the 1975 referendum. More than anyone else, Heath was responsible for bringing Britain into Europe.

JUNE 1975

WHAT HAPPENED AFTER BRITAIN JOINED EUROPE?

The arguments about whether or not to join the European Community (EC) had been mainly about the economy – jobs, prices, food, trade and especially access to the 'Common Market'. But the EC itself was changing fast and soon Britain's membership was about much more than money.

EUROPE SPREADS ITS WINGS

By the 1970s, the European Community was already starting to develop an environmental policy – trying to clean up the air, rivers and seas by cutting down pollution from industry. Later on, European countries began to work together to protect consumers and to improve people's rights in the workplace. The EC started giving help to poorer countries around the world. Eventually there was co-operation to fight crime and even the beginnings of an European army.

VOTING FOR EUROPE

At the same time, the democratic side of Europe was growing. In 1979, just four years after Britain joined, the first direct elections to the European Parliament were held. Now British citizens could vote for their representatives in Europe and have a say in decisions made in Brussels. The Parliament gained more powers over the years, although many people felt it was still not enough.

Inside the chamber of the European Parliament in Brussels. Elections are held every five years in 28 countries. There are currently 751 Members of the European Parliament (MEPs).

EUROPE GETS BIGGER

At the same time as the EC was taking on new areas of work, it was getting much bigger. Southern countries Greece, Portugal and Spain joined in the 1980s in the 'Mediterranean expansion'. The borders of the EC moved north in 1995 when Sweden and Finland joined (along with Austria). After the fall of Communism in Eastern Europe in 1989, the newly democratic countries there were keen to join. Eventually 11 of them did – although it took many years to achieve this.

A NEW NAME

Twenty years after Britain joined, Europe was no longer just a Common Market – it was moving towards being a state in its own right. It had a flag, an anthem, a parliament, a foreign policy and it was planning its own currency – the Euro. To reflect all these changes, under the Maastricht Treaty of 1992, the European Community changed its name to the European Union – the EU.

The EU has gradually expanded from just six members to 28. Only a few European countries – including Norway, Switzerland and Iceland – have stayed outside.

1957

1973

1981

1986

1995

2004

2007

2013

WHAT WERE THE PROS AND CONS OF BRITAIN'S MEMBERSHIP?

As the European Union developed, there were many benefits for ordinary citizens in all the member countries – but there was a financial cost for Britain and not everyone was happy.

LIVING AND WORKING ABROAD

British citizens now had the right to live and work in any other EU country. Learning a foreign language and adapting to another culture could be difficult, but qualifications and experience gained in one country were now recognised in another. It became a lot easier to buy property in another EU country as a holiday home, or to retire abroad. Plenty of older people headed off to Spain or France and bought a place in the sun where they could still receive their British pensions.

Retirement in the sun was a dream for many Britons. The EU helped make it a lot easier for those dreams to come true.

LIVING ABROAD

By 2011, there were 900,000 British citizens living in other EU countries: most of them were of working age. Spain, France, Ireland and Germany were the most popular countries.

STUDYING IN OTHER COUNTRIES

Starting in 1987, the EU offered opportunities for students to study or gain work experience in another European country, through the 'Erasmus' programme. By 2017, more than 300,000 British students had taken part: for most of them, it was their first experience of living in another country.

TRAVEL WITHOUT BORDERS

In 1995, the Schengen Agreement abolished border controls and passport checks between nearly all EU countries. Britain decided to keep border checks – worrying that it would be too easy for criminals and illegal migrants to enter the country. However, it became much easier to travel within the EU for everyone.

Crossing the German border. Note that there are no passport controls or even a German flag, just the yellow stars of the EU.

LOOKING AFTER CONSUMERS

For those travelling to, or living in, other EU countries, there were many useful benefits. The European Health Insurance Card meant people could easily get medical treatment in another country. The EU did its best to protect people on holiday, for example, by giving compensation to those delayed at airports and by reducing mobile phone charges.

RIGHTS IN THE WORKPLACE

With EU citizens, including British ones, free to work in any member country, there was a need to have the same protection for all workers. The EU helped improve health and safety at work, gave people better pension rights, and set a minimum of four weeks holiday every year. European laws also helped bring more equality for women in the workplace.

HELPING THE REGIONS

Starting in 1975, the EU began to help the poorer regions of Europe catch up with the richer areas. For example, EU money was spent on building better roads, training workers in new skills and helping people to set up new businesses. In Britain, Wales and Cornwall were the areas that most benefitted – the Highlands of Scotland, Northern Ireland and parts of northern England also did well.

Cronfeydd yr UE:
Buddsoddi yng Nghymru

Ewrop & Chymru:
Buddsoddi yn eich dyfodol
Cronfa Datblygu Rhanbarthol Ewrop
★ ★ ★
★ ERDF ★
★ ★ ★
Europe & Wales:
Investing in your future
European Regional Development Fund
Llywodraeth Cymru
Welsh Government

EU Funds:
Investing in Wales

↑ A new road in Wales built with EU money. Billions of pounds were spent by the EU in poorer regions, including over £2 billion a year in Britain.

THE COST OF EUROPE

Despite the money coming into some regions, Britain as a whole ended up paying much more into the EU than it got back in return. As poorer countries joined the EU, Britain became the biggest contributor, along with Germany. Margaret Thatcher, British Prime Minister in the 1980s, famously managed to negotiate a refund of part of Britain's money. But the high cost of being in the EU was still unpopular.

RULES AND REGULATIONS

On top of the cost of Europe, EU laws now took priority over laws made by the British Parliament. Some of these laws were welcomed – for example, those trying to clean up beaches and protect wildlife. But others were seen as adding costs and extra paperwork to businesses and farmers.

Sheep grazing at Stonehenge in Wiltshire. British farmers were now part of a single system to control agriculture right across Europe.

COMPETITION ALL ROUND

British firms had many extra opportunities to do business in EU countries. But at the same time, firms from all over Europe could sell in Britain, take over British companies, and supply the government with goods and services. Fishermen and farmers got payments from the EU under the 'Common Agriculture Policy', but they also faced new competition.

DIFFERENT IDEAS OF EUROPE

There were many advantages to be being in the EU. But more than any other country, Britain came into conflict with Brussels – over money, borders, rules and regulations, and who should make the laws within Europe. Usually a compromise was found, but trouble was brewing for the future.

THE CHOCOLATE WAR

Sometimes it seemed easier for European firms to succeed in Britain than the other way round – people complained about a lack of 'fair play' by some EU countries. For example, it took 27 years before British chocolate could be sold in the EU!

WHY DID BRITAIN DECIDE TO HOLD A VOTE ON BREXIT?

After the Maastricht Treaty in 1992, there were constant battles over Europe in Britain, especially within the Conservative Party.

BATTLES BEGIN

Under this Treaty, the EU was planning to become more like a single state with its own currency, foreign and defence policy and a single EU citizenship. Britain had reservations and Parliament only just approved the Treaty. For the next five years, Conservatives who were against Maastricht made life very difficult for the then Prime Minister, John Major.

UKIP GETS GOING

In 1993, the same year that Maastricht came into force, the UK Independence Party (UKIP) was founded. UKIP aimed to take Britain out of the EU and bring back control over all laws from Brussels to London. At the time, no-one paid much attention to UKIP, but over the next 20 years, it gradually built up support.

The new Euro currency was introduced from 2002. Britain decided not to join the Euro – another sign of differences between London and Brussels.

MOVING TO BRITAIN

After 2004, when the eastern European countries joined the EU, many people decided to use their new rights to move to Britain to live and work. Jobs in Britain were much better paid than in, say, Poland or Romania. Later on, more joined them from southern European countries such as Greece, Spain and Italy – particularly young people who could not find work at home.

The number of people arriving was much more than had been expected – 3.2 million people from elsewhere in the EU eventually moved to Britain, about five per cent of the population.

CHEAPER STAFF

Immigration brought many benefits to Britain. For example, farmers could find workers to pick fruit and vegetables, and restaurants and bars could employ cheaper staff. Better-off people had Polish plumbers, Bulgarian gardeners and Portuguese childminders. But others were unhappy. They felt wages were being forced down by the new arrivals and there were even complaints that some companies refused to employ British workers.

A Pret a Manger sandwich bar. In 2012, the company was attacked for having no British staff at some branches, and it promised to try harder to recruit them. Five years later, it was still struggling to do so.

EU CITIZENS IN BRITAIN: TOP FIVE COUNTRIES (2015)

POLAND	916,000
IRELAND	332,000
ROMANIA	233,000
PORTUGAL	219,000
ITALY	192,000

TOASTERS AND BANANAS

At the same time as more European workers arrived in Britain, rules and regulations made in Brussels were getting more and more unpopular. Among the products that the EU tried to control were the shape of bananas and the power of toasters. Some of the stories in the newspapers about EU regulations were exaggerated, but people were left with the impression that Brussels was trying to control everyday life.

↑ The EU did not actually ban 'bendy bananas', as some people claimed, but it did try to control their shape and quality.

EUROSCEPTICS

This word was used to describe people (and also newspapers and political parties) who were critical of the EU; a sceptic is someone who is doubtful or questioning. For a long time, Eurosceptics were seen as a small minority who were overly worried about Europe. But later on, 'Euroscepticism' became widespread in Britain.

FINANCIAL WORRIES

The idea that joining the EU would solve Britain's money worries had not really turned out to be true. Under the Single Market (the new name for the Common Market), European countries were selling far more to Britain than British companies sold to them. On top of that, Britain was still paying much more money into the EU than it got back.

To make things worse, the new Euro currency was not working very well. The economic crisis was giving the EU a bad name, with high unemployment and poverty in countries such as Greece and Spain.

COUNTRIES PAYING THE MOST INTO THE EU (2015)
. . . .

1. GERMANY
2. BRITAIN
3. FRANCE
4. THE NETHERLANDS
5. ITALY

Protestors against European economic policies outside the parliament in Athens, Greece. Financial trouble in various countries gave the EU a bad name.

CAMERON GOES FOR A VOTE

All these concerns about the EU helped UKIP to win more support and in 2014, it came first in the European Parliament elections, getting more votes than any other party. Conservative Prime Minister David Cameron knew that many of his own party were unhappy about the EU and wanted a referendum on whether or not to stay in. Worried about the rise of UKIP, he promised to make a new deal between Britain and Brussels and hold an 'In/Out' referendum if the Conservatives won the 2015 election.

Cameron's promise calmed the situation and helped the Conservatives win the election. Now he had to carry it out.

WHO WERE THE PEOPLE FOR AND AGAINST BREXIT?

Cameron's new deal with Brussels included some limits on immigrants' rights and a promise that Britain could stay out of the Euro. Now it was time for the British people to vote on whether to 'Leave' the EU or 'Remain' in it.

The referendum campaign started in February 2016. Very quickly, two campaign groups were set up, separate from the political parties – the Leave Campaign (sometimes called the 'Brexiteers') and the Remain Campaign (often known as the 'Remainers'). Most politicians supported Remain.

NIGEL FARAGE – LEAVE

The leader of UKIP was the most famous face of the 'Leave' campaign. With a pint of beer in his hand, he gave out a man-of-the-people image. He felt it was his life's work to take Britain out of the EU.

BORIS JOHNSON – LEAVE

The colourful Conservative and ex-Mayor of London made a big difference to the vote when he came out in favour of leaving the EU. 'Boris' was particularly popular among young people.

BREXIT

DAVID CAMERON – REMAIN

As Prime Minister, David Cameron was leading the campaign to stay in the EU. He thought his new deal with Brussels was a good one, but it did not change the big problems and few people understood it. Cameron had a reputation as a lucky politician who always won elections, but perhaps he was over-confident.

NICOLA STURGEON – REMAIN

The First Minister of Scotland, leader of the Scottish Nationalists, was passionately in favour of staying in. She was joined on the 'Remain' side by the Liberal Democrats, the Welsh Nationalists, the Green Party and nearly all parties in Northern Ireland.

JEREMY CORBYN – REMAIN

Labour Party leader Jeremy Corbyn was in favour of staying in the EU. But at the same time, he had his own personal doubts about the way Europe was going, particularly for workers' rights. Some people felt he did not campaign hard enough for 'Remain'.

THERESA MAY – REMAIN

The future Prime Minister was Britain's Home Secretary at the time. She was in favour of 'Remain', but kept a low profile during the campaign. Once Britain had voted, she accepted the result and worked to make Brexit happen – her low profile actually turned out to be quite helpful in her rise to be Prime Minister.

BUSINESSES

Businesses were divided about the referendum. Most big firms and the City of London (Britain's financial and banking centre) were in favour of Remain. Some of these companies wrote to their staff warning that jobs could be lost if Britain voted to leave. But others, particularly smaller businesses, were fed up of EU regulations and wanted to Leave.

MORE AUSTERITY OVER BREXIT FEARS

ONE MARKET MILLIONS OF JOBS

open-britain.co.uk

OPEN BRITAIN

YOUNG? YOUR COUNTRY NEEDS YOU

⬆ People demonstrating for Remain in Trafalgar Square. Jobs within the Single Market were one of Remain's best arguments.

YOUNG PEOPLE

Young people were much more active in favour of Remain. Many felt that leaving the EU would take away the opportunity for them to live, study or work abroad in the future.

OLDER PEOPLE

Support for Leave was strongest among older people. Some remembered the first referendum way back in 1975 and felt that the EU had gone well beyond what they had signed up to then, which had been just a Common Market.

CELEBRITIES

Actors, pop stars, sports personalities and celebrities were generally more likely to support Remain, although some did get behind Leave, such as Sol Campbell and Sir Michael Caine. David Beckham, JK Rowling and Bob Geldof were among those who urged people to vote Remain.

BRITISH PEOPLE ABROAD

Some British people living abroad were able to vote by post. Many of those living in EU countries were worried about losing their rights to work or use local health services if Britain left and so most were in favour of staying in.

THE MEDIA

By law, the BBC and other television channels were supposed to give both sides of the argument during the campaign. The newspapers were not limited in the same way: some papers supported Remain, but important ones with many readers were for Leave. For example, *The Sun, The Daily Mail* and *The Telegraph* attacked the EU continuously and had a lot of influence.

LIKES FOR LEAVE

On social media such as Facebook, Twitter and YouTube, the country was divided. But research later showed that the Leave campaign was more successful than Remain in using social media to make its arguments.

Newspaper front pages from the day of the Brexit vote. Many of the most popular papers were strongly in favour of Brexit.

WHAT WERE THE ARGUMENTS DURING THE CAMPAIGN?

The Remain campaigners chose to talk mainly about jobs and the economy, while on the Leave side the biggest themes were immigration and bringing back power from Brussels to London.

'PROJECT FEAR'

The official slogan of the Remain campaign was 'Britain Stronger In Europe'. Led by David Cameron, they warned that if Britain voted to leave, jobs would be lost, taxes would have to go up, British companies would find it difficult to trade in Europe and the economy would crash. Everyone would be poorer: each household stood to lose £4,300 a year.

Remain supporters also claimed that terrorists would find it easy to get into Britain if there was no co-operation with the EU and even that war would be more likely.

In general, the Remain campaign argued that leaving the EU was too risky, and did not have much to say about the positive side of being in Europe. As a result, their campaign was criticised for being 'Project Fear'.

The Bank of England was among the many organisations warning about the financial risks of Brexit.

OBAMA GETS INVOLVED

Other countries also urged the British against voting for Brexit. The popular US President Barack Obama visited London and pleaded with voters not to support Leave. He warned that it would not be easy for Britain to make a trade deal with America in the future if it was outside the EU.

RULES AND REGULATIONS

While the Remain campaign was full of warnings, Leave supporters stressed the benefits of being free of EU rules and regulations. They reminded people of the many stories over the years about Brussels 'interfering' in everyday life. Brexit, they argued, would set people and companies free of these costly regulations.

Leave campaigners also wanted to bring decisions back to Britain from Brussels. They argued that democracy had been damaged by allowing the EU too much power. National 'sovereignty' – the ability of a country to control its own affairs – had been lost. That was why their slogan was 'Take Back Control'. It sounded a lot more dynamic than 'Britain Stronger In Europe'.

> Sometimes these EU rules sound simply ludicrous, like the rule that you can't recycle a teabag, or that children under eight cannot blow up balloons, or the limits on the power of vacuum cleaners.
>
> • • • • • •
>
> **Boris Johnson, article in _The Telegraph_, 16 March 2016**

A fleet of small fishing boats take to the River Thames outside Parliament in support of Brexit. Many fishermen were unhappy with EU rules.

25

MONEY FOR THE NHS?

On top of arguments about regulation, the Leave campaign claimed that Britain would save a lot of money by leaving the EU. They suggested that millions of pounds could be diverted to the National Health Service (NHS). These claims were disputed and Leave was accused of lying about their figures. Later some of the Leave campaigners admitted they had made a mistake. But the idea that the EU was expensive had already stuck in many people's minds.

The controversial bus belonging to the Leave campaign, which travelled around the country with the message that an extra £350 million a week could go to the National Health Service if Britain left the EU.

ARGUING OVER MIGRATION

One of the biggest issues of the campaign was immigration and border control. Pictures of refugees, for example in Greece or Calais, had been on TV screens almost continuously for over a year. Knowing that many people felt too many migrants had come into Britain, the Leave campaign promised that immigration would fall if Britain left the EU.

They warned that if Britain stayed in, Turkey would eventually join the EU and 76 million more people would have the right to live and work in Britain.

Some felt the language used by certain Leave campaigners was offensive and racist: they believed Britain should be a welcoming country, especially to refugees. A poster used by the Leave campaign showing refugees was reported to the police. Nigel Farage was especially criticised.

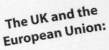

INFORMATION ABOUT THE REFERENDUM ON 23 JUNE 2016

The UK and the European Union:

THE FACTS

HM Government

Why the Government believes that voting to remain in the European Union is the best decision for the UK.

The EU referendum, Thursday, 23rd June 2016.

ON THE CAMPAIGN TRAIL

The referendum campaign was fought just like any election in Britain. There were millions of leaflets put through people's doors, posters in the streets, demonstrations and rallies, public meetings to debate Brexit, and huge coverage in the media. Both sides spent heavily on advertising, but political broadcasts on television were free. Thousands of volunteers knocked on people's doors to try and persuade them to vote one way or the other. In total, £32 million was spent on the campaign.

David Cameron tries to persuade people to vote Remain in a live debate for Facebook and BuzzFeed news.

JUNE 2016

WHAT WAS THE RESULT?

On Thursday 23 June 2016, more than 26 million people around the country went to vote in the Brexit referendum.

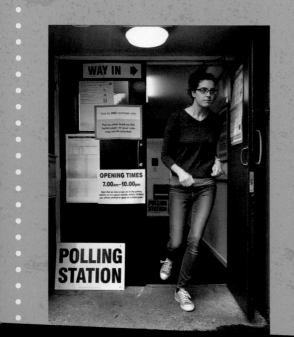

GOING TO THE POLLS

People voted in polling stations set up for the day, usually in schools or community centres. Voting hours were from 7 a.m. to 10 p.m.. It was also possible to vote by post and more than seven million people chose to take part that way. After 10 p.m., the vote count started. Counting was a long process involving thousands of people and so the results only started to be known in the middle of the night.

UK AS A WHOLE

Across the whole country, Leave won by 51.9 per cent to 48.1 per cent. That meant 17.4 million people for Leave and 16.1 million people for Remain. Just over seven out of ten people who were allowed to vote actually did.

⬆ Leaving a polling station after voting. Only people over 18 and registered to vote could take part.

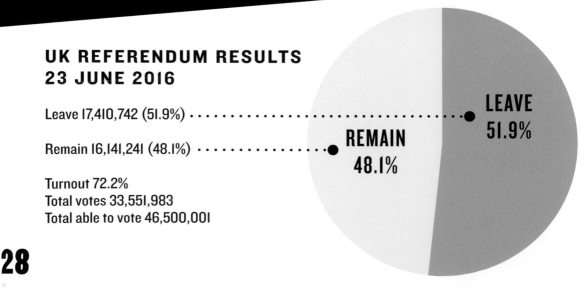

UK REFERENDUM RESULTS 23 JUNE 2016

Leave 17,410,742 (51.9%) ·

Remain 16,141,241 (48.1%) · · · · · · · · · · · · ·

Turnout 72.2%
Total votes 33,551,983
Total able to vote 46,500,001

REMAIN 48.1%

LEAVE 51.9%

HOW BRITAIN VOTED

SCOTLAND
Scotland was strongly against Brexit. Remain won by 62 per cent to 38 per cent. Every single area of Scotland without exception voted for Remain.

NORTHERN IRELAND
Northern Ireland was in favour of staying in the EU. Remain got 55.8 per cent of the vote, and Leave 44.2 per cent.

WALES
People in Wales voted for Brexit in similar proportions to England. The score was 52.5 per cent for Leave and 47.5 per cent for Remain. Cardiff and some parts of mid-Wales voted Remain.

Gibraltar

ENGLAND
England was in favour of Brexit. Leave got 53.4 per cent and Remain 46.6 per cent. Every region of England, apart from Greater London, voted to Leave. Some of the big cities such as Leeds, Manchester and Liverpool also voted for Remain, but most smaller towns and country areas were in favour of Leave.

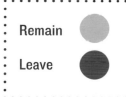

Remain

Leave

WHY DID PEOPLE VOTE THE WAY THEY DID?

The result showed that dire warnings about the cost of Brexit from the Remain campaign were not believed by many people. Leave won because immigration and the wish to take back control from Brussels were seen as more important than the economy.

TAKING BACK CONTROL

Warnings from big businesses, the Bank of England and top politicians about leaving the EU did not impress many ordinary people. On the contrary, they felt that the EU had mainly benefitted the rich and powerful, the same people who were now telling them to vote Remain. Some Leave voters knew there would be a price to pay for getting out of the EU, but went ahead and voted leave anyway – to them, it was more important that Britain got back control of its borders and its sovereignty.

A PROTEST VOTE?

Controlling immigration into Britain was a big theme of the campaign. Many Leave voters saw the referendum not just as a chance to protest against past immigration, but the only way to stop more people entering the country in the future.

Migrants hoping to come to Britain at a refugee camp in Calais, France. Fear of further immigration played a big role in Brexit.

BETTER OFF OUT?

The claim by the Leave campaign that more money would be spent on the National Health Service if Britain left the EU was important in persuading people to vote for them. It may not have been a completely true claim, but many people believed it. To them, it was a real example of 'Better Off Out', which was one of the main slogans used by Leave.

GOING A DIFFERENT WAY

Scotland voted differently to England and Wales: strongly for Remain. One reason was the strength of the Scottish National Party, which had always been pro-Europe. The popular First Minister, Nicola Sturgeon, helped convinced Scots to vote to stay in the EU. Some Scottish people also felt the Leave campaign was dominated by English nationalists. In Northern Ireland, people were used to travelling freely across the border and trade between the Republic of Ireland and the North was important. So a majority voted for Remain.

Supporters of Remain gather outside the Scottish Parliament in Edinburgh, waving EU and Scottish flags.

OLD AND YOUNG

Older people were more likely to vote for Brexit: two out of three of those over 65 did so. On the other hand, the younger generation was in favour of staying in: three out of four of those under 25 voted Remain. The problem for the Remain campaign was that too few young people actually went out to vote. Some had not registered to vote in time.

⬆ Older people tended to support Leave, younger Remain, but more older people voted.

BETTER LEADERSHIP

Leaders of the Leave campaign such as Nigel Farage and Boris Johnson put in stronger performances. By contrast, David Cameron struggled to convince people. Labour Party leader Jeremy Corbyn was criticised for campaigning poorly. Although Labour was in favour of Remain, many traditional supporters of the party turned to Leave – they were worried about immigration and felt closer to Farage and UKIP.

STAYING AT HOME

Even though the Brexit referendum was one of the most important decisions ever taken in Britain, more than 13 million people did not vote – a quarter of the population. Some were on holiday, away from home or simply too busy working. Others had no interest in politics or felt that the vote would not make any difference to their lives.

WHAT WAS THE IMMEDIATE REACTION?

Very few people in politics and the media had been expecting Leave to win and the result was a big shock. Many people struggled to even believe it had happened.

DELIGHT AND DESPAIR

While the Remain campaigners were in despair, Brexit supporters were delighted. Nigel Farage gave a victory speech and then went to celebrate, naturally with a pint of beer.

JUNE 2016 Nigel Farage was happy with the referendum result. Soon afterwards, feeling his job was done, he resigned as leader of UKIP.

> " This will be a victory for the real people, for the ordinary people. Let June 23 go down in history as our Independence Day.
>
> • • • • • •
>
> **Nigel Farage, speech, 24 June 2016** "

THE POUND TAKES A DIVE

The first reaction was in the financial markets of the City of London. The value of the British pound immediately fell sharply. Some businesses were very nervous and started to make plans to leave Britain. There was a sense of panic for a short while, but gradually things returned to normal.

CAMERON SAYS GOODBYE

On the day after the Brexit vote, David Cameron resigned as Prime Minister. He had gambled on the referendum to settle the long-running problem of Britain's relations with the EU – but he had lost his gamble. Soon afterwards, he left politics altogether.

Cameron was quickly replaced by Theresa May as Britain's leader. She had been in favour of Remain, but now she promised to carry out the wishes of the people as voted in the referendum. 'Brexit means Brexit,' she famously said.

May gave important jobs to several of the Leave campaigners, including Boris Johnson, who became Foreign Secretary. It was now up to the leading figures of the Leave campaign to prove their argument that Britain would be better off out of the EU.

> " The British people have made a choice, that not only needs to be respected but those on the losing side of the argument – myself included – should help to make it work.
>
> • • • • • •
>
> **David Cameron, resignation speech, 24 June 2016** "

A grim-faced David Cameron gives his resignation speech in Downing Street the morning after the result. His wife, Samantha, stands by.

SCOTLAND IS ANGRY

Scotland had been the country most strongly in favour of Remain. People there were unhappy with the result, and the question of Scottish independence from the rest of the United Kingdom was now being discussed again. Nationalists felt independence was the way for Scotland to stay in the EU.

EUROPE IS SHOCKED

Many politicians in other European countries could hardly believe that the British had decided to leave – most leaders felt it was a sad day for Europe and were worried for the future of the EU. However, some were relieved that the long-running arguments between Britain and the other countries about borders, money and trade would now be coming to an end.

Eurosceptic politicians in countries such as France and the Netherlands, on the other hand, were pleased with the result. They wanted to see the end of the EU, or at least big changes in how it was run, and now hoped for referendums in their own countries.

European leaders meet to discuss how to react to Brexit, without Britain being there.

TWO YEARS' WAIT

Europeans living in Britain feared they might have to leave the country or lose their jobs straightaway. However it soon became clear that very little was going to change for at least two years – the minimum time it would take the British government to negotiate a legal exit of the EU.

WHAT DID PEOPLE DO TO TRY TO STOP BREXIT HAPPENING?

Once the shock of the referendum result died down, some people tried to stop Brexit happening – on the streets, in the courts, and in Parliament.

TAKING TO THE STREETS

In the months after the vote, there were several large demonstrations against Brexit. The protestors hoped to persuade politicians to change their minds – it was known that a majority of Members of Parliament were not in favour of leaving the EU.

The British people had voted to Leave, but the result had been very close. So some people wanted a second referendum to be held. They felt that the country had been misled by the Leave campaign and hoped to change people's minds before a new vote.

JULY 2016

Thousands join an anti-Brexit march in London just after the vote, still hoping that Brexit would not be carried out.

Anti-Brexit campaigner Gina Miller speaking to the media outside the High Court in London. She won her case but Parliament still voted in favour of Brexit.

NOV 2016

THEIR DAY IN COURT

In order to make sure Brexit was voted on in Parliament, a group of citizens went to the High Court in London. They were led by Gina Miller, an investment manager, and Deir Dos Santos, a Brazilian-born hairdresser. After several court cases, in January 2017 the Supreme Court judges decided Parliament must vote on whether Brexit could go ahead.

PARLIAMENT VOTES

Now those who were against Brexit had a hope. But most MPs, even those who were originally against Brexit, felt that the will of the people, as expressed in the referendum, must be respected. There were long debates in Parliament but finally the law applying Brexit was passed on 13 March 2017.

MAY SIGNS THE LETTER

Other European countries were beginning to get impatient for Britain to finally make up its mind. They had their wish on 29 March when Prime Minister Theresa May officially wrote to Brussels giving notice under Article 50 of the Maastricht Treaty that Britain would leave.

'REMOANERS'

The court cases and the debates in Parliament held up the process of starting Brexit for many months. Those who had voted in favour of Leave were frustrated, attacking those who tried to block Brexit as 'Remoaners' – people who moaned about the referendum result. Britain was still very divided about Brexit.

37

WHO WILL BE AFFECTED BY BREXIT?

Europeans living in Britain and Britons living abroad are the most concerned about Brexit. But all businesses and individuals will be affected in some way.

TIME TO RELOCATE?

For the 3.2 million people from other EU countries living in Britain, life may change completely. The same is true for the 900,000 British citizens around Europe. If no agreement is found to cover living and working abroad, many may have to give up their jobs and return to their home countries.

SHORT OF WORKERS?

Because of the number of EU citizens working in Britain, many parts of the economy may suffer if large numbers of people have to leave. For example, farmers depend on people from eastern Europe to pick fruit and vegetables. Health service workers including doctors and nurses often come from other European countries. Universities too have many international staff.

Health service staff show their support for staying in the EU during the Brexit referendum campaign.

HIGHER PRICES?

The value of the British pound has fallen against the Euro since Brexit. This means higher prices for food and drink that is imported from the EU. Holidays in Europe will get more expensive too. All in all Britain imports more than it exports and so the cost of living is likely to go up for everyone.

CITY OF LONDON

Banks and financial companies in the City of London are very important for the British economy, earning money from around the world, providing many jobs and paying a lot of taxes. But to keep doing business with the EU, these firms may have to move to other cities elsewhere in Europe – such as Dublin, Paris or Frankfurt. London could lose its position as the financial capital of Europe, as well as many highly paid jobs.

Skyscrapers in the City of London. Many financial workers may have to move to other countries as a result of Brexit.

NORTHERN IRELAND

Northern Ireland is especially affected by Brexit because it is the only part of the United Kingdom that has a land border with the EU. And that border is generally open. A special agreement will have to be found, otherwise people's lives may be disrupted.

A massive container ship being unloaded at Felixstowe, Britain's biggest port. International trade talks will decide whether Brexit is a success or failure.

SINGLE MARKET

After 2019, British businesses will no longer have access to the European Single Market. A new trade agreement will have to be made, otherwise all sides will lose out. For example, it would be harder for the French to sell wine, or for the Germans to sell cars, to the British. Equally, British companies selling to Europe could suffer new taxes on their products and as a result many people might lose their jobs.

On the other hand leaving the EU may give Britain more opportunities to trade with fast-growing countries outside Europe, such as China and India. New trade deals could also be made with the USA and English-speaking countries such as Australia. Businesses in Britain could be freed from some of the EU rules and regulations they have complained about.

WHO WILL BE AFFECTED BY BREXIT?

> "I believe the UK is in a prime position to become a world leader in free trade because of the brave and historic decision of the British people to leave the European Union.
>
> • • • • • •
>
> **Liam Fox, International Trade Minister, speech in Manchester, 29 September 2016**

FARMING AND FISHING

Growing food and catching fish have been almost totally controlled by the EU ever since Britain joined in the 1970s. With Brexit, a new system will now have to be created, particularly as farmers get much of their income from the EU and fishermen are limited as to how much fish they can catch by agreements in Brussels. It will not be easy to create a new system after so many years.

WHAT NOW FOR STUDENTS?

The possibility to study abroad has been one of the big successes of EU membership. No-one yet knows if British students will be able to continue to study in other European countries after Brexit, nor how easy it will be for European students to come to Britain.

Students by a canal in Amsterdam, the Netherlands. Studying abroad may get more difficult for the British. ⬇

WHAT HAPPENS NEXT?

The first real talks between Britain and the other EU countries began in June 2017. There are less than two years – up until March 2019 – to agree the details about how Britain will leave.

DIVORCE PAYMENT

Leaving the EU has been compared to a couple getting divorced: there are usually arguments over money. The EU wants Britain to pay for some of the promises it had made in the past, for example the pensions of British staff in working in Brussels.

Britain on the other hand feels that it should not have to pay. Because Britain is no longer in the EU 'club', it should not have to pay a 'membership fee'.

To make things more complicated, the EU will have a gap in its budget once Britain leaves. Therefore it wants to get as much money as possible from Britain. The British government, on the other hand, knows that one reason people voted for Brexit was due to the cost of the EU. So it would be very unpopular to agree to a big 'divorce bill'.

OCT 2016 All smiles as new Prime Minister Theresa May meets the head of the EU, Jean-Claude Juncker, in Brussels. But the talks ahead might not be so friendly.

European Commission

CITIZENS' RIGHTS

The other 27 countries are determined that their citizens living in Britain can continue to stay after 2019. Britain is concerned about Britons living around Europe. An agreement will have to be found that covers living and travelling abroad. In the same way, a new trade deal will have to be made.

All in all, the future is very uncertain after Brexit. If Britain and the other 27 countries can make a fair deal quickly, life could carry on without too much trouble. If not, there could be chaotic scenes at the ports and airports, with long queues for people and goods to get in and out of Britain.

Both Britain's leaders and the EU leaders say they want to remain close friends. But only time will tell if that is possible.

> "
> The UK wants to leave and pay nothing. It's not possible. There must be a threat, there must be a risk, there must be a price.
> . . . . . .
> **Former French President François Hollande, 6 October 2016**
> "

> "
> No deal for Britain is better than a bad deal for Britain.
> . . . . . .
> **Prime Minister Theresa May, January 2017**
> "

Waiting to get into Britain at Heathrow Airport. Queues may get a lot longer if a good deal is not made between Britain and the EU.

TIMELINE

1945 World War Two ends

1946 Winston Churchill calls for a United States of Europe

1951 The European Coal and Steel Community is set up involving
six countries

1957 Under the Treaty of Rome, the European Economic Community
(EEC) is founded by six countries

1963 French President de Gaulle turns down Britain's application
to join the EEC

1967 De Gaulle says 'no' to Britain for a second time

1973 Britain finally joins the EEC under Conservative Prime Minister
Edward Heath

1975 New Labour Prime Minister Harold Wilson calls a referendum –
Britain votes by a 2 to 1 margin to stay in the EEC

1979 First direct elections to the European Parliament

1984 Prime Minister Margaret Thatcher wins a reduction in Britain's
payments to Europe

1989 Fall of the Berlin Wall and the end of communism in Eastern Europe.
The following year, Germany is reunited.

1993 The Common Market becomes the European Single Market

1993 Under the Maastricht Treaty, the EC becomes the European Union (EU).
In Britain, the UK Independence Party (UKIP) is founded.

1995 The Schengen Agreement comes into force, allowing EU citizens
to travel without border controls

2002 The Euro comes into use as a single currency in 12 EU countries
and others prepare to follow. Britain does not.

2004	Ten new countries, mainly from eastern Europe, join the EU. Immigration to Britain starts to increase dramatically.
2014	UKIP wins the European Parliament elections in Britain
APRIL 2015	David Cameron promises a referendum on 'Brexit' if his Conservative Party wins the General Election
JUNE 2015	After being re-elected, Cameron begins talks in Brussels with other countries about changing's Britain's relations with Europe
FEBRUARY 2016	With the EU talks over, Cameron calls a 'Remain' or 'Leave' vote on Brexit
23 JUNE 2016	Britain votes by 52% to 48% to leave the European Union
24 JUNE 2016	David Cameron resigns as Prime Minister
13 JULY 2016	Theresa May takes over from Cameron
24 JANUARY 2017	The Supreme Court rules that May must get permission from Parliament to start Brexit
13 MARCH 2017	Parliament passes the law on Brexit
29 MARCH 2017	Theresa May formally writes to the EU giving two years' notice that Britain will leave (Article 50)
8 JUNE 2017	British General Election – Theresa May and the Conservatives lose their majority but she stays on as Prime Minister
19 JUNE 2017	Negotiations begin between Britain and the other 27 EU countries
29 MARCH 2019	This is the date on which the UK is expected to leave the EU

GLOSSARY

BREXIT – short for 'British exit' or Britain leaving the European Union (EU)

'BREXITEER' – slang word for a person in favour of leaving the EU

BRITISH EMPIRE – the group of countries around the world controlled by Britain in the past, including Canada, Australia and India. Member countries gradually gained independence and the Empire ended in the 20th century.

BRUSSELS – capital of Belgium and home to the European Parliament. Most EU decisions are made in Brussels.

COMMON AGRICULTURAL POLICY – the system of paying farmers across the EU to make sure that the Europe had enough food

COMMON MARKET – one of the original names for the EU. Within a Common Market, all countries can buy and sell their goods without having to pay extra taxes. Later the Common Market became known as the Single Market.

COMMUNISM – the system of government used in eastern Europe and Russia from 1945 to 1990. The government controls the economy and there are no free elections.

DEMOCRACY – the system used in Britain and other EU countries where the government is voted in (or out) by the people

EEC – European Economic Community, an earlier name for the EU between 1957 and 1974

EC – European Community, an earlier name for the EU between 1974 and 1993

EU – European Union, the name was used from 1993 onwards

EUROSCEPTIC – a person generally against the EU and wanting Britain to leave it

REFERENDUM – a vote of the people to decide whether or not a country should choose to do something, for example should Britain stay in, or leave, the European Union

REGULATIONS – detailed rules made by the EU covering, for example, how products should be made

'REMAINER' OR 'REMOANER' – slang words for a person in favour of staying in the EU

SINGLE MARKET – another term for Common Market

SOVEREIGNTY – when a country has full control over its own laws, it is said to be 'sovereign'

SUPREME COURT – the highest court of the land in Britain

TREATY – a legal agreement between two or more countries, for example the Treaty of Rome in 1957, which started the EEC

FURTHER INFORMATION

Here are some other books and websites you might want to look
at to find out more about the European Union and Brexit:

BOOKS

Britain and the European Union: A comprehensive guide for children
by Simon Adams and Simon Ponsford (Franklin Watts, 2016)

Young Explorer: Brexit – Britain's Decision to Leave the EU by Daniel Nunn (Raintree, 2016)

Raintree Perspectives: What Does It Mean to Be British? by Nick Hunter (Raintree, 2016)

WEBSITES

europa.eu/european-union/about-eu_en
This link is to 'About the EU' on the European Union's official website.

europa.eu/kids-corner/index_en.htm
This link is to 'Kid's Corner' on the European Union's official website
which includes games and quizzes.

www.voteleavetakecontrol.org/index.html
This is the official website of the Vote Leave campaign.

www.strongerin.co.uk/
This is the official website of the Vote
Remain campaign.

INDEX